Close-Up C1

WORKBOOK KEY & RECORDING SCRIPT

Unit 1

Reading

1C 2D 3A 4B 5C 6D 7C 8A 9B
10C 11D 12B

Vocabulary

A
1b 2a 3c 4a 5c 6b

B
1 discrimination
2 accomplishments
3 persistence
4 failure
5 achievements
6 understanding
7 realisation
8 adaptability

C
1 positive
2 conceited
3 defeated
4 modest
5 impetuous
6 upbeat
7 apprehensive
8 headstrong
9 breakthrough
10 went for it
11 triumphant
12 generations

D
1 get ahead
2 come up against
3 fallen through
4 hang on
5 blown away
6 knuckle down
7 pull off
8 break through

E
1 light
2 places

3 up
4 mile
5 hitch
6 get
7 do
8 plate

T0349597

Grammar

A
1 has been painting
2 freezes
3 've just finished
4 's always forgetting
5 drives
6 Have you been waiting
7 'm revising
8 've never disagreed

B
1 He's just left
2 We've been camping
3 I've just heard
4 Susan hasn't received
5 We're really looking forward
6 How are you getting on
7 Jenny never hands
8 Anthony is always complaining

C
1 had decided
2 fell
3 set up
4 had been
5 hadn't been sleeping
6 was shaking
7 were
8 stampeded
9 explained
10 found

D
1c 2b 3c 4c 5b 6a 7c 8a

E
1c 2h 3b 4e 5g 6f 7a 8d

Listening

?c 3a 4b

ing

2T 3T 4F

B
1 To whom it may concern
2 Yours faithfully

Unit 2

Reading

1c 2a 3b 4d

Vocabulary

A
1 choice
2 contact
3 personal
4 views
5 legitimate
6 updated
7 identity
8 click

B
1 remark
2 observed
3 offended
4 criticism
5 avoided
6 relates
7 value
8 resist

C
1 criticism
2 defence
3 reaction
4 accesible
5 bothering
6 provocation
7 excitement
8 shocking

1

D
1 aback
2 to
3 for
4 at
5 out
6 in
7 up
8 down

E
1c 2b 3c 4a 5c 6b 7a 8c

Grammar

A
1 Shall I bring
2 will be revising
3 will have finished
4 will have been writing
5 will manage/is going to manage
6 am going to look
7 fly
8 will enjoy

B
1 will have peaked
2 will become
3 will sound
4 will continue
5 are going to expect
6 won't be able to follow
7 will be moving
8 will have realised

C
1 Shall I carry
2 will have been married
3 I'll go
4 we arrive
5 we're driving
6 will have been working
7 I'm not going to/I won't help you anymore!
8 I'll be sunbathing

D
1b 2f 3d 4a 5e 6c

E
1 will have been living
2 will be late
3 will still be tidying up
4 are meeting
5 soon as you've finished your homework
6 were going to meet up
7 they were starting their journey
8 he would apply to medical school

Listening
1 paper
2 sound

3 declining
4 outweigh
5 hooked
6 French
7 upgrading
8 beach

Writing

A
Tick **1, 2, 4, 5, 7, 8**

B
1 Secondly
2 Thirdly
3 As a result
4 However
5 though
6 Nevertheless

Review 1

Vocabulary

A
1c 2b 3a 4d 5c 6b 7a 8d 9c
10c 11a 12d 13b 14c 15a 16d
17a 18b 19b 20d

Grammar

B
1c 2a 3c 4d 5c 6d 7b 8c 9c
10b 11a 12c 13d 14a 15c 16c
17d 18b 19c 20a

Use of English

C
1d 2a 3b 4d 5d 6a 7d 8a 9b
10b 11a 12c

D
1 off
2 ahead
3 without
4 through
5 against
6 warning
7 all
8 by
9 in
10 did
11 occasion
12 on
13 there
14 break
15 away

E
1 access
2 confidence
3 guess
4 horse
5 construction

F
1 took my words out of context
2 say it to your face/tell you to your face
3 aren't up to scratch
4 got a lot on my plate
5 get the green light
6 was taken aback by
7 work around the clock
8 not to get back at

Unit 3

Reading
1D 2F 3B 4E 5C

Vocabulary

A
1 mixed
2 oblivious
3 muscular
4 forgetful
5 nutritious
6 beneficial
7 bony
8 treatment

B
1 relieved
2 psychological
3 emotional
4 anorexic
5 intravenous
6 dehydrated
7 physical
8 undernourished
9 monitored
10 recovered

C
1b 2a 3c 4b 5a 6c 7a 8b

D
1 running
2 coughing
3 bodily
4 failing
5 internal
6 terminal
7 chemical
8 splitting

E
1c 2f 3e 4a 5d 6b

Grammar

A
1 herself
2 Those
3 nothing

4 each other
5 Anyone
6 one another's
7 these, those
8 all

B
1 something
2 herself
3 Everyone
4 Some
5 Others
6 yourself
7 Nothing
8 someone

C
1 never
2 with her aunt and uncle
3 tomorrow
4 in three weeks
5 to get rid of my headache
6 incredibly

D
1 absolutely
2 wide
3 hard
4 uncomfortably
5 highly
6 Unfortunately
7 Strangely
8 late

E
1 desperately
2 late
3 high
4 carefully
5 utterly
6 highly
7 fast
8 lately

Listening
1c **2**d **3**b **4**d **5**a **6**c

Writing
A
1F **2**T **3**T **4**F

B
1 Comfortable clothes
2 A great night's sleep
3 Essential stuff
4 Health and safety

Unit 4

Reading
1b **2**c **3**b **4**b **5**a **6**d

Vocabulary
A
1 groundbreaking
2 heart-rending
3 agent
4 film editor
5 producer
6 lines
7 usher
8 stage

B
1 show
2 foyer
3 usher
4 row
5 intermission
6 act
7 aisles
8 backstage

C
1c **2**b **3**a **4**b **5**a **6**b **7**c **8**c

D
1 performance
2 Animated
3 lead
4 role
5 rehearsals
6 portrayal
7 fright
8 ovation

E
1e **2**c **3**g **4**a **5**f **6**h **7**b **8**d

Grammar
A
1 not giving
2 to buy
3 Acting
4 hurry
5 to go
6 watching
7 to bring
8 to let

B
1 see → seeing
2 to watch → watching
3 to go → going
4 see → to see
5 to do → do
6 playing → to play
7 be → being
8 to lose → losing

C
1a **2**c **3**b **4**c **5**c **6**b **7**a **8**a

D
1 in fact
2 As a matter of fact
3 Evidently
4 apparently
5 obviously
6 quite honestly
7 Anyway

E
1c **2**f **3**b **4**a **5**d **6**e

Listening
1e **2**g **3**a **4**d **5**c **6**e **7**h **8**c **9**b
10a

Writing
A
1 people interested in the theatre/plays and shows
2 a theatre production
3 No, they aren't theatre.
4 No, you need to choose something you liked and would recommend.

B
1b **2**f **3**e **4**c **5**a **6**d

Review 2

Vocabulary
A
1c **2**a **3**d **4**c **5**b **6**a **7**c **8**c **9**d
10b **11**b **12**a **13**c **14**d **15**c **16**c
17b **18**a **19**d **20**d

B
1b **2**c **3**d **4**a **5**b **6**c **7**d **8**b **9**a
10d **11**c **12**d **13**b **14**a **15**c **16**b
17c **18**d **19**d **20**b

Use of English
C
1c **2**d **3**a **4**d **5**d **6**b **7**b **8**c **9**a
10b **11**c **12**a

D
1 bodily
2 imbalance
3 dehydrated
4 thirsty
5 internal
6 undernourished
7 fright
8 heartstrings
9 disorders
10 headaches

E
1 mixed
2 talk

3 lead
4 notice
5 play

F
1 an actor by profession
2 putting on an act
3 remained/was still in character
4 overcame all (the) obstacles
5 had a change of heart
6 at the top of his lungs
7 always/constantly at each other's throats
8 bite my head off

Unit 5

Reading
1a 2c 3b 4d

Vocabulary

A
1 appetite
2 quench
3 culinary
4 cuisine
5 resist
6 pile
7 simmer
8 shed

B
1E 2C 3E 4T 5T 6C 7T 8C

C
1 banquet
2 helping
3 ravenous
4 mouldy
5 scrumptious
6 starved
7 salty
8 sip

D
1c 2b 3b 4a 5c 6b 7a 8b

Grammar

A
1 dined out
2 passed out
3 gulp down your juice/gulp your juice down
4 has come down with (the) flu
5 the sale fell through
6 will get ahead in her career
7 picked at his dinner
8 tucked in

B
1 fight it off
2 polish them off
3 keep up with her
4 warm it up
5 came up with it
6 get away with it

C
1 have
2 shall
3 would
4 is
5 would
6 is
7 did
8 could

D
1 she would
2 do you
3 that is
4 she should
5 would you
6 do you
7 they aren't
8 I do

E
1 I'm going to stick to a low-carb diet from now on, **I am.**
2 correct
3 Max hasn't got any time to cook at the moment, **he hasn't.**
4 I don't suppose I could use your espresso machine, **could I?**
5 correct
6 correct
7 correct
8 I'm sure I brought the biscuits home with me, **I am.**

Listening
1c 2b 3b 4c 5b 6a 7b 8c

Writing

A
1 the college principal
2 formal or semi-formal
3 four
4 one of the menus

B
Suggested answers
Introduction: The purpose of this proposal is to recommend a menu for the Leaver's Dinner.
Conclusion: I can't recommend the Mediterranean choice highly enough. Although widespread and popular, it will still seem special, festive and memorable.

Unit 6

Reading
1B 2F 3D 4E 5A

Vocabulary

A
1b 2f 3d 4a 5c 6e

B
1 endure extreme weather conditions
2 trigger a landslide
3 absorb oxygen
4 emit carbon dioxide
5 spew ash and magma
6 harness energy

C
1 steep
2 searing
3 narrow
4 barren
5 sweltering
6 breezy
7 hostile
8 harsh

D
1 unreliable
2 sufficient
3 migration
4 surrounding
5 elements
6 insistence
7 alternative
8 indifferent

E
1 down
2 up
3 up
4 up
5 down
6 over

Grammar

A
1 needn't
2 couldn't
3 would
4 should
5 must (should)
6 Can/Could
7 mustn't/can't
8 might/may/could

B
1 May I leave now
2 needn't lock your doors here
3 can't be at home
4 could take the train

5 is bound to be late
6 don't have to buy tickets in advance
7 should read this publication
8 must be somewhere in

C
1 must have finished
2 may have left/might have left
3 needn't have worried
4 could have given/would have given
5 can't have tidied
6 shouldn't have gone/ought not to have gone

D
1 must have become
2 would have thrown
3 must have starved
4 would have spewed
5 could have survived
6 might have been
7 wouldn't have been able
8 may have spread

E
1b **2**e **3**c **4**a **5**d

Listening
1b **2**a **3**c **4**b

Writing
A
1F **2**T **3**F **4**T

B
1 aims
2 thrive
3 include
4 disposing
5 to saving
6 to improve

Review 3

Vocabulary
A
1c **2**a **3**d **4**b **5**b **6**c **7**d **8**a **9**c
10c **11**d **12**b **13**b **14**c **15**a **16**d
17c **18**a **19**d **20**b

Grammar
B
1c **2**d **3**a **4**d **5**c **6**a **7**b **8**c **9**a
10c **11**b **12**d **13**a **14**b **15**c **16**b
17d **18**a **19**c **20**b

Use of English
C
1c **2**b **3**c **4**d **5**a **6**b **7**b **8**d **9**d
10a **11**b **12**a

D
1 would
2 have
3 up
4 clear
5 down
6 against
7 on
8 would
9 into
10 but
11 life
12 bound/likely/able
13 by
14 of
15 it

E
1 whip
2 feed
3 skim
4 spill
5 chain

F
1 must have been bucketing down for
2 might not have known
3 mustn't interfere with
4 a complete/total waste of time
5 could have polished off all (of)
6 no use crying over spilt milk
7 put up with him
8 must wake up and smell the

Unit 7

Reading
1E **2**G **3**B **4**A **5**D **6**E **7**C **8**F **9**G
10D

Vocabulary
A
1b **2**c **3**b **4**a **5**b **6**c **7**b **8**a

B
1 automation
2 purity
3 assembly
4 corrosion
5 displacement
6 computerised
7 replacement
8 assumptions

C
1 material
2 process
3 substance
4 properties

5 hardness
6 artificial
7 gemstone
8 industry

D
1 home page
2 recycle bin
3 search engines
4 double click
5 hard drive
6 laser printer
7 memory stick
8 control panel

E
1f **2**c **3**e **4**a **5**d **6**b

Grammar
A
1 hadn't got
2 won't pass
3 could help
4 would still be
5 would have got
6 had never invented
7 would be
8 mix

B
1 if
2 unless
3 as long as
4 provided
5 won't
6 Supposing
7 otherwise
8 would
9 If
10 could

C
1e **2**a **3**h **4**c **5**g **6**b **7**f **8**d

D
1 Hannah wasn't always late
2 he had revised for the test
3 I were a musician/I could be a musician
4 he were/was going on holiday with his friends
5 you would do the washing-up

E
1 Not only is this book extremely long, but it's also very boring
2 Nowhere will you find a more patient teacher.
3 Rarely were we allowed to do experiments when we were children.
4 Not until I was thirty was I able to afford a car.

5 No sooner had they got to the beach than they ran into the sea.
6 Under no circumstances are you to lift this by yourself as it's much too heavy.

Listening

1 mobile phones
2 financial
3 transparency
4 cheaper
5 reality
6 reunite
7 weather
8 genuine

Writing

A

1 the editor and other journalists working for the college science magazine
2 a medical researcher
3 No, they can be from any century.
4 formal language

B

2, 4, 1, 3

Unit 8

Reading

1c 2d 3a 4c 5d 6b

Vocabulary

A

1 dollars
2 cash
3 money
4 pounds
5 bank teller
6 forgeries
7 counterfeit
8 currency

B

1 fraudulent
2 broke
3 withdraw
4 laundering
5 economical
6 poverty
7 recession
8 rating

C

1d 2a 3f 4e 5b 6c

D

1 on
2 in

3 back
4 out
5 out
6 down

Grammar

A

1d 2h 3f 4c 5a 6j 7i 8g 9b 10e

B

1b 2c 3c 4a 5b 6a 7b 8a

C

1a 2f 3e 4b 5d 6c

D

1 going out
2 Having saved
3 Being
4 Having inherited
5 ordered
6 Having survived

E

1 What
2 All
3 thing
4 reason
5 where
6 when

Listening

1a 2b 3b 4a 5c 6c 7a 8b 9a
10c 11b 12c 13a 14b

Writing

A

1 college students primarily
2 semi-formal
3 the pros and cons of online auctions

B

1st main paragraph: what you like about online auction websites
2nd main paragraph: what you dislike about online auction websites
3rd main paragraph: the effect of online auction websites on conventional shops

Review 4

Vocabulary

A

1b 2c 3d 4a 5a 6c 7b 8b 9c
10d 11a 12d 13c 14b 15b 16a
17d 18c 19d 20b

Grammar

B

1c 2b 3a 4d 5a 6c 7c 8a 9c
10b 11d 12d 13c 14a 15d 16c
17b 18d 19c 20a

Use of English

C

1 for
2 who
3 no
4 than
5 had
6 would/might
7 Having
8 on
9 which
10 Being
11 then
12 worth
13 when
14 edge
15 out

D

1 billionaires
2 prosperous
3 trader
4 leading
5 economic
6 loss
7 downgrade
8 financial
9 statement
10 savings

E

1 effective
2 wires
3 money
4 chip
5 panel

F

1 light years ahead of
2 it isn't rocket science
3 who throws money around
4 reason (that/why) he's wealthy is
5 1883 is the year (that)
6 at cost price
7 push the panic button
8 hadn't tried to reinvent

Unit 9

Reading

1C 2D 3A 4D 5B 6F 7A 8E 9B
10E 11F 12C

Vocabulary

A

1b 2c 3a 4c 5b 6c 7c 8a

B

1 movement
2 controversy
3 portrait
4 commissions
5 landscapes
6 oil
7 canvas
8 subjects

C

1 reproductions
2 exhibition
3 culmination
4 performance
5 opening
6 backing

D

1 mainstream
2 tour
3 display
4 debut
5 contract
6 vocalist
7 heart
8 management

E

1e 2c 3g 4a 5h 6f 7b 8d

Grammar

A

1 I don't think Lady Gaga is a **more** talented singer than Katy Perry, do you?
2 correct
3 correct
4 Mary felt she wasn't **as** gifted a musician as her sister.
5 Those paintings aren't as impressive **as** you'd imagine.
6 correct
7 They're not **such** expensive tickets as I'd thought they'd be.
8 correct

B

1 much worse than
2 a bit shorter than
3 considerably fewer than
4 a great deal less popular than
5 a lot less interesting than
6 far more bands than

C

1 the most important
2 the largest
3 (the) best known
4 as vibrant
5 longer
6 bigger
7 more sprawling
8 the most entertaining
9 the most visited
10 best loved

D

1 serious enough
2 too tired
3 quietly enough
4 talented enough
5 too lazy
6 too late
7 enough paintings
8 too famous

E

1 such, positive
2 such, flop
3 so long
4 So complex
5 so easy
6 Such, determination

Listening

1b 2c 3c 4a 5d 6b

Writing

A

1F 2F 3T 4F

B

1 privileged
2 Artistically
3 simplicity
4 improvement
5 attention

Unit 10

Reading

1c 2c 3a 4a 5d 6c

Vocabulary

A

1 cosmopolitan
2 sedentary
3 formative
4 rigorous
5 provincial
6 pricey
7 solitary
8 hectic

B

1 struggling
2 juggling
3 enduring
4 balancing
5 concerned
6 spoiling
7 excelled
8 outdone

C

1 metropolitan
2 Obsessive
3 active
4 irritable
5 susceptible
6 addictive
7 unsophisticated
8 sociable

D

1c 2e 3b 4g 5a 6h 7f 8d

E

1 hit rock bottom
2 came up against
3 safe and sound
4 burn the candle at both ends
5 ruined your chances
6 wear down
7 throwing in the towel
8 do without

Grammar

A

1 are you being overlooked
2 aren't you being promoted
3 you haven't been chosen
4 not being noticed
5 dealing with
6 to be seen
7 to deliver
8 is recognised
9 are identified
10 wasn't built

B

1 was given to the most deserving person
2 is known that there aren't any more opportunities for growth this year
3 are expected to be made
4 I got for the meeting have been eaten
5 was decided that our groups would be merged
6 schools are expected to close early

C

1 appears to have lost
2 seems to be getting
3 appear to have left
4 seems (to be)
5 appears to be improving/ appears to have improved
6 seems to have disappeared

D

1. painted
2. decorated
3. stuck
4. dyed
5. removed
6. broken
7. cleaned
8. ruined

E

1. appears to have been/can be resolved
2. seem to have adapted/that they are
3. doesn't seem to have listened to/seem as if she's followed
4. seem to have really meant it/seem as if/like you're very keen
5. seem to have forgotten that you promised/your promise/to be reading it
6. appears to have done/seems that every dish in the house has been used

Listening

1E 2H 3B 4D 5F 6D 7F 8A 9H 10C

Writing

A

1DK 2F 3T 4F 5T

B

1. hustle and bustle
2. peace and quiet
3. friendlier
4. drawbacks
5. inadequate
6. surrounded

Review 5

Vocabulary

A

1b 2d 3c 4c 5a 6b 7c 8c 9b 10a 11c 12b 13d 14d 15c 16a 17c 18b 19d 20a

Grammar

B

1b 2a 3c 4a 5d 6b 7c 8b 9d 10c 11a 12c 13b 14d 15b 16a 17c 18b 19c 20d

Use of English

C

1d 2a 3b 4a 5d 6b 7d 8b 9c 10a 11a 12b

D

1. without
2. down
3. the
4. bottom
5. say
6. against
7. ground
8. if/though
9. back
10. as
11. such
12. by
13. changing
14. throw
15. above

E

1. opening
2. chart
3. spoilt
4. field
5. stroke

F

1. would be music to my ears
2. aren't enough places to sit
3. need the stage curtains to be
4. long as to put people
5. the more expensive the tickets will
6. having her paintings put on
7. were so few participants (that)
8. was so confusing a project (that)

Unit 11

Reading

1b 2c 3d 4a 5a 6c

Vocabulary

A

1. hindrance
2. coverage
3. dazzling
4. Conducting
5. holder
6. dedication

B

1. cheered
2. applause
3. relay
4. lap
5. baton
6. obstructed
7. disqualified
8. ban

C

1. off
2. for
3. up
4. back
5. out
6. up
7. out
8. on

D

1a 2b 3c 4a 5b 6b 7b 8c

Grammar

A

1e 2f 3a 4e 5b 6d

B

1. forget to bring your trainers tomorrow
2. 'll train for an hour every day until you're
3. I join the basketball team next term
4. we put away the equipment now
5. 'll meet you at the pool at eight tonight
6. bring me your

C

1. offered to help me put up
2. advised me to warm up before I started
3. decided not to get the green sweatshirt
4. promised to be there at 10.30
5. complained that Stella always arrived too late
6. apologised for missing
7. encouraged me to join
8. warned me not to overdo the stretches

D

1. if/whether I had brought my
2. why he wasn't playing football
3. when Rob was going on
4. Sarah how she was getting
5. if his son's team had won
6. Vincent if/whether he knew where the team was staying
7. his mother where his tennis racket was
8. Rose wanted to know why Tina didn't like

Listening

1c 2b 3b 4a 5c 6b

Writing

A

1. Simon Perez
2. tell him the principal has asked you to reply

3 two: one about facilities in the college and another about facilities in town
4 semi formal as Simon is a young student, but you don't know him

B
1 regarding
2 delighted
3 instructor
4 Additionally
5 available
6 charge
7 satisfactory
8 forward

Unit 12

Reading
1C 2F 3D 4A 5E

Vocabulary
A
1 killing
2 holds
3 shape
4 predict
5 hunch
6 pockets

B
1 speculate
2 guess
3 eternity
4 omen
5 posterity
6 infinite

C
1 likely
2 anticipated
3 looming
4 critical
5 intended
6 preserve

D
1c 2a 3f 4d 5b 6e

Grammar
A
1c 2e 3h 4b 5g 6a 7f 8d

B
1b 2a 3c 4b 5c 6a 7b 8b

C
1 worked very hard/because she wanted to go to law school
2 is so much competition/find/are finding it very difficult

3 to budget cuts/won't renovate/be renovating
4 so many decisions to make very quickly/surprising that Camilla is feeling
5 to price rises/unlikely to be able
6 that/as you handed in/you can't expect

D
1 Either
2 either of
3 Neither
4 nor
5 either
6 Neither of

E
1d 2g 3c 4h 5f 6a 7e 8b

Listening
1 crust
2 hot springs
3 heat and cool
4 transfer
5 melt
6 wells
7 the United States
8 export

Writing
A
1F 2T 3T 4F 5T

B
1b 2d 3c 4a

Review 6

Vocabulary
A
1b 2a 3d 4c 5c 6a 7b 8d 9c
10b 11a 12d 13b 14c 15c 16a
17d 18b 19a 20c

Grammar
B
1d 2c 3c 4d 5b 6b 7a 8c 9a
10d 11a 12b 13c 14d 15c 16a
17b 18c 19c 20a

Use of English
C
1 fanatics
2 burning
3 observers
4 overpower
5 maniacs
6 disqualified
7 commentator
8 referee

9 sharpen
10 captivating

D
1 holds
2 the
3 next
4 seeing
5 as
6 in
7 of
8 off
9 for
10 since/as/because
11 to
12 even
13 so
14 spite
15 being

E
1 shape
2 secret
3 dropped
4 lap
5 hold

F
1 Neither George nor Paul
2 fell at the first hurdle
3 apologised for not making it to
4 if he had practised that
5 congratulated Karen on her
6 made a killing signing with
7 Next to travelling in space, nothing
8 should watch the launch the following

RECORDING SCRIPT

Unit 1

You will hear two different extracts. For questions 1-4, choose the best answer, a, b or c. There are two questions for each extract.

Extract One
You will hear two people on a music programme talking about a new CD.

M	So, now on to Bobby Miller's latest CD, just out this week. What are your first impressions?
W	Well, if I'm completely honest, and, er, if you consider all the hype surrounding it, I'd have to say I'm less than impressed.
M	Yeah, me too. I was expecting more …
W	The thing is, his first CD was just brilliant. It was so innovative and refreshing and, well … it was full of potential, wasn't it? Then his second CD came out and I've got to admit I liked it, though it did feel a tad samey.
M	Yeah, and now of course, it's just more of the same again. It's OK, but the freshness is gone. He really needs to find a new angle. His songs are becoming indistinguishable …
W	I couldn't agree more. There's also the issue with some of the other band members. I don't think they're really that committed any more. They just seem to be going through their paces.
M	Yeah, I know what you mean, like they're thinking of something else while they're playing … They look so bored onstage these days … Having said all that, are you going to buy the CD?
W	Ah, yeah, well, I've already bought it, so yeah…

Extract Two
You will hear part of a radio interview with a man who has just swum across the English Channel.

W	Congratulations, Richard. How did you feel when you finally stood on the beach in France after eleven hours and ten minutes in the water?
M	Well, mostly I would say what I felt was relief. I couldn't believe I'd made it. I also felt absolute joy at finally fulfilling my dream – I've wanted to swim the Channel since I was a kid. And of course, I'm really grateful to everyone who sponsored me. We've managed to raise over ten thousand pounds already for a worthy charity.
W	You said before you set off that your main worry was the cold.
M	Definitely. The channel is bitterly cold, as cold as 15°C, which is really, really cold when you compare it to your local pool, which is more like 30°C.
W	Wow! I hadn't realised that. That is very cold.
M	It sure is. You know, I wasn't really worried about the distance, as I'd been training for at least three hours every day for the last year. No, it was the cold I was concerned about. But in the end, that wasn't the biggest challenge. It was the quantity of ships crossing the Channel that was our biggest headache. They are a real hazard.
W	Yes, I can imagine there are lots of ferries …
M	Up to one hundred a day just between Dover and Calais. And don't forget commercial ships – hundreds

of them – so it's incredibly busy. If you're in their way, that's it really. But my team were fantastic. They kept me fed and watered and made sure I was well out of the way of any vessels … It's funny, though, because no one had foreseen the jellyfish. They look creepy, but when you're in a wetsuit as I was, they can't do you much harm.

Unit 2

You will hear someone talking about her views on an aspect of technology. For questions 1-7, complete the sentences.

I must admit I was reluctant to get an e-book reader when they first came out. My first thought was that this was the beginning of the end of publishing as we know it and that paper books would, little by little, become a thing of the past.

Loving books as much as I do – their feel, their smell, even their sound as you turn the pages – this was the last thing I wanted. Imagine your bookshelves empty, with just one e-book reader or tablet computer on it instead of the colourful paperbacks and beautiful hardbacks of our childhood?

What's interesting, though, is how quickly I was converted. It's true, lots of people are now reading mainly on their e-book readers or tablet computers. And yes, sales of paper books are declining as sales of e-books rise. Indeed, my fears weren't unfounded. But in the end, I think the benefits of the new technology outweigh the disadvantages.

What changed my mind? Well, I was given an e-book reader for my birthday and I have to confess I was hooked from day one. I've already downloaded a dozen free classics and am reading all the novels I meant to read in my youth. What is more, as I have access to dictionaries in any language you can think of, I've started reading in French again. When I don't know what a word means, I just touch it and up pops the definition. Magic!

So, what's the result? I'm reading much more than I ever used to. I'm watching less television and spending less time surfing the net. And I'm not the only one. I've noticed my daughter is reading more too. She has a tablet computer though, which is much more sophisticated than my e-book reader.

I would also like to think that by reading e-books instead of paperbacks, I might be helping to save the planet. That is the theory, of course, but the reality is that I only will if I refrain from upgrading, which is going to be hard. As faster, more powerful, smaller and more sophisticated e-readers and tablet computers come on the market, will I be able to resist getting the latest model? I'm not sure. Does this mean we'll be seeing mountains of outdated e-readers piling up in landfill? I hope not, but only time will tell.

In the meantime, I'm a convert. The only time I read a paper book now is at the beach, as I wouldn't want to get sand in my precious e-reader.

Unit 3

You will hear a radio interview about flu pandemics. For questions 1-6, choose the best answer, a, b, c or d.

INT Welcome to today's edition of *Check up*. Our special guest this afternoon is epidemiologist Andrew Law, who's going to talk to us about influenza, or flu. Welcome, Andrew.

A Thank you. It's great to be here.

INT First of all, Andrew, can you tell us a bit about your job, about epidemiology?

A Yes, yes of course. Well epidemiologists like me study diseases in the community. Our aim is to find out where diseases come from, how they spread, what they do and of course, how we can prevent them. We are concerned with epidemics like flu and cholera, but also with problems like obesity and heart disease.

INT Obesity and heart disease? Surely they don't behave in the same way as influenza. They aren't really contagious, are they?

A No, you're right, they aren't, not like flu. Flu is extremely infectious. It's mainly transmitted from person to person. In fact, it is an airborne virus. This means that you can catch it by being near someone who is coughing and sneezing, and also from touching something that has been sprayed with droplets from coughing and sneezing. You can even catch it from having a conversation with an infected individual.

INT And obviously, obesity can't be caught in this way.

A Exactly, although it does tend to run in families, so you could say it is transmissible in a way …

INT That's true … But going back to flu, can you tell us a little more about it? Everyone knows about the devastating Spanish flu pandemic just after World War I, in 1918-1919. And, more recently, the swine flu pandemic in 2009 …

A Actually, people call it swine flu, but we don't think the 2009 pandemic was caused by pigs at all. It seems more likely that it was caused by a mutation of swine, avian (that's birds) and human flu viruses. Unfortunately, calling it swine flu ended up causing a great deal of unnecessary hardship, as governments panicked and forced farmers to slaughter thousands of perfectly healthy pigs …

INT I didn't know that. That's awful. So people didn't catch it from being close to pigs.

A No, the vast majority of people will have caught it from other people infected with the virus.

INT So it spread in the usual way …

A Precisely.

INT So, Andrew, am I right in thinking that the 2009 flu pandemic started in Mexico City and lasted around eighteen months, killing fewer than 20,000 people?

A Actually, that's not quite right. The first person to have been diagnosed with this new strain of influenza virus, 'patient zero', was a boy in Veracruz, in eastern Mexico. But scientists think it more likely that the virus emerged the year before. As for fatalities, we believe now that the figure of eighteen and a half thousand deaths caused by swine flu, or to be more precise, by the H1N1 virus, was a gross underestimation. Research has now shown that the figure is more likely to be somewhere between three hundred and six hundred thousand deaths. The problem is that it's impossible to keep an exact count of every single case. Also, people don't always recognise the cause of death, especially in less developed countries.

INT Yes, I can imagine. But three hundred to six hundred thousand is a huge number.

A It is indeed. But having said that, it is nowhere near the catastrophic outcome of the Spanish flu pandemic of 1918, which is known to have killed no fewer than twenty-five million people, though some researchers believe the number to be somewhere between fifty and one hundred million.

INT That's incredible. So Spanish flu killed many more people than World War I.

A There's no doubt about it. Of course, you've got to remember there weren't any vaccinations then and people weren't as aware of how diseases like influenza spread. Today, we know what precautions to take and we can produce a vaccination for a new strain of flu in a matter of months, if not weeks. Healthcare education campaigns have also had a huge influence. Just making sure you wash your hands properly with soap and water every time you come home, especially after being in a crowded space, like a bus or a train, makes an enormous difference.

INT And covering your mouth, using a tissue, whenever you cough or sneeze.

A That's right. We've come a long way …

Unit 4

You will hear five people talking about their roles in film, cinema and TV. Complete both tasks as you listen.

Task 1 For questions 1-5, choose from the list A-H the person who is speaking.

Task 2 For questions 6-10, choose from the list A-H what each person is expressing.

Speaker 1
What can I say? It's the perfect job for someone like me. I just adore showing off, pretending to be someone else. It comes naturally, you know. And now that we're doing the new series of *Kansas* for Channel 8, I've got work for the next two or three years. As a matter of fact, my only problem now is that people recognise me when I go out shopping. The other day, I forgot why I'd gone to the supermarket. I just spent all my time signing autographs. Don't get me wrong, I'm not complaining. I love it, really.

Speaker 2
Well, things could be going better, I suppose. It's not that I mind the job, really. I like dressing up, after all, and I know I look smart in my uniform. And of course, I get to see so many celebrities, opening the door for them, helping them with their bags … And now and then, I do go for the odd audition. No luck, no, not yet. But, yeah, the job is fine – a bit cold sometimes of course – and always on my feet, but the tips are pretty good, so all in all, I can't complain …

Speaker 3
I still can't believe it, to be honest. Sometimes, I just think surely there must be some kind of mistake and I'm going to wake up to find out it was all just a dream. But, no, here I am working on set in New Zealand, transforming actors into orcs, hobbits and wizards. Admittedly, it's hard work. Can you imagine, sometimes it can take two or three hours to do someone's makeup, especially if they need a huge nose or lots of scars, for example. But the actors are all so professional and we do get to know them quite well. They're really good fun. All in all, it's a dream come true …

Speaker 4

After years directing films and TV shows, it gives me enormous pleasure to be back in the theatre where I started off so many years ago. Actually, I had always believed my life would be spent there … In other words, I never imagined moving to California and hanging out with movie stars, let alone directing them in blockbusters! But all that is over now. I've come back to my first love and can't wait to direct Shakespeare plays once more …

Speaker 5

I have to confess, I'm disappointed with this one. It was always going to be hard designing for such a period when you're used to the twentieth and twenty-first century. I just wish we'd had more time to research it properly. Having said that, I think the peasants look convincing on the whole. The rough cotton and wool we sourced look just right on the big screen. Actually, it's the noblemen's costumes I'm not that pleased with. Some of the fur really does look fake and now that I know a bit more about the period, I realise that we got some of the details wrong. Some of the colours wouldn't have been available in the Middle Ages … Quite honestly, I'd rather forget about this film and just get on with the next one.

Unit 5

You will hear eight short conversations. Choose the best answer, a, b or c that means about the same thing as you hear or that is true according to what you hear.

1
M I can't find the butter. I'm quite sure I bought some, but now it's disappeared!
W Let me have a look. Here it is! See? Just behind the cheese.
M Oh! Well, how am I supposed to find things when you're always hiding them?

2
M Where have you been? I was really worried.
W Were you? I sent you a text to tell you I was having dinner at Annie's.
M You did, did you? Let me see … Oh, yes, I see, here it is. Sorry … I should have checked my messages.

3
M So, you're going to train as a chef, are you?
W Yes, I decided that there was no point carrying on at school. I've always wanted to have my own restaurant.
M Well, one step at a time.

4
W Oh, dear, poor Henry has really piled on the pounds.
M I know. He's always been on the large side, but now I suppose he'd be classified as clinically obese.
W Well, I just hope he does something about it.

5
M Did you know, there weren't any tomatoes in Europe before the Spanish explorers brought them back from the New World in the fifteen hundreds?
W Wow, that's amazing. I knew chocolate came from Mexico, from Mesoamerica, I should say, but I didn't realise tomatoes did too.
M Yeah, and chilli peppers, avocados, vanilla and don't forget potatoes.

6
W You look fantastic. How long have you been dieting?
M Actually, I'm not really on a diet. I've changed my eating habits, you see. Instead of living on fast food, I've started cooking. It's incredible! I'm never hungry, and the weight has just fallen off.
W Well, it's really worked. You look great.

7
W How about fish and chips tonight? Or maybe a curry?
M No. Seriously. We had pizza last night and Chinese the night before. We can't live on takeaways.
W So you're going to cook, are you?
M OK. I suppose a curry isn't that bad for you …

8
W You can't go on like this. Eating on the hoof, never sitting down for a proper family meal.
M You're right, I know. It's just that I've had so much on my plate recently, what with work and exams. But as soon as they're over, I'm going to change my ways.
W Well, I'll believe it when I see it …

Unit 6

You will hear two different extracts. For questions 1-4, choose the best answer, a, b or c. There are two questions for each extract.

Extract 1
You will hear two people talking about bush fires.

W Did you hear the news this morning, about all those terrible bush fires in Australia?
M Yes, I did. It's awful.
W I hadn't realised they were so common, though, had you?
M Actually, I do know a bit about them. There were a lot of fires in California when I was living there.
W Really? But were they started by people? Or are they a natural phenomenon, caused by drought and heatwaves? It was forty-five degrees in Australia, and it hadn't rained for ages, so the conditions were perfect for bush fires.
M Well, if I remember rightly, statistics show that four out of five fires are in fact caused by people. It's incredible that such carelessness, dropping a cigarette or not putting out a fire properly, can cause such disasters.
W Oh, it can't be four out of five, surely. That can't be right. Still, these days people do manage things much better don't they? It's brilliant the way firefighters fight fire with fire, you know, starting fires in a controlled way to get rid of undergrowth and ground litter from the forest floor. This means that when there is a big fire, there *is* less to burn so they aren't as destructive.
M That's true. But you also need to realise that fires are essential for the health of a forest. They return nutrients to the soil by burning dead or decaying matter. They also act as a disinfectant, burning diseased plants and harmful insects from a forest ecosystem. And by burning through thick canopies and bushy undergrowth, wildfires allow sunlight to reach the forest floor, so a new generation of seedlings can grow. All this helps keep the forest in good shape.
W So they are in fact a necessary evil, really …

Extract 2

You will hear two people discussing the habits of the parasitic emerald cockroach wasp.

W It's an extraordinary discovery, I must say. If you thought it was only humans that are obsessed with hygiene, then think again. We now know that there is a wasp that has developed its own food hygiene techniques. And here is our guest, entomologist Dr Stonehouse, who is going to tell us some more about this extraordinary insect.

M Thank you so much. Yes, well … The study that has been done has revealed that this wasp, the parasitic emerald cockroach wasp has developed a way of cleaning its food with a cocktail of antimicrobial liquids.

W And why does it need to do this?

M: Well, you see, the cockroach wasp actually lays its eggs, one egg to be precise, on the leg of an American cockroach. It's rather gruesome, but what happens is this: when the egg hatches, the larva bores a hole in the cockroach and moves inside.

W Quite horrible, yes.

M Yes, indeed. It goes on to feed on the internal organs of the cockroach. But before it does this, it secretes an antimicrobial liquid from its own body that literally coats the cockroach in a sort of antiseptic soup and makes it safe to eat.

W How extraordinary! But why does the wasp larva do this?

M Well, we all know cockroaches live in pretty unsanitary conditions – they are full of viruses, microbes and fungi, so if the larva didn't do this, it would pick up all sorts of diseases when it ate the cockroach. It wouldn't survive, in fact. It's incredible, but the chemicals in the larva's secretions – mullein and micromolide – are just the right substances needed to kill off the bacteria commonly found in American cockroaches. So once it's given it a good clean, the wasp larva can eat it all up safely.

W Incredible!

Unit 7

You will hear a presentation about how technology is changing the lives of people in Africa. Listen and complete sentences 1-8.

M And now Georgina will present her report.

W Thanks, Luke. My report is about how mobile phones have changed the lives of people in Africa over the last decade, focussing on seven different areas: banking, activism, education, entertainment, disaster management, agriculture and health.

Let's look at banking first: Many Africans now use mobile money to pay their bills, buy goods and make payments to individuals. Remittances from relatives living abroad are also largely done via mobile banking, and in some African countries more than half the adult population uses mobiles to make financial transactions, according to the Gates Foundation and the World Bank.

Next, activism: One lesson from the 2011 uprisings across North Africa was that mobile phones, with their infinite opportunities for connection and communication, are able to transform disenchanted citizens into resistance fighters. Across the continent mobile phones are also bringing unprecedented levels of openness and transparency to the electoral process.

Education is another key area: The potential for transforming the continent's dysfunctional educational system is immense, as mobile phones, which in comparison to PCs are cheaper to own and easier to run, gain ground as tools for delivering teaching content. It is hoped that this will help reduce the significant numbers of school-age African children who are not receiving any formal education.

As well as changing the face of education, mobile phones have had a huge effect on entertainment. A 2009 survey found that 'entertainment and information' were the most popular activities for which mobile phones are used in Nigeria, in particular for dialling into favourite radio shows, voting in TV reality shows, downloading and sharing songs, photos and videos, as well as tweeting.

They are proving invaluable, however, when it comes to disaster management. The organisation, Refugees United, for example, has teamed up with mobile phone companies to create a database where refugees can register their personal details. The information available on the database allows them to search for people they've lost contact with and is now helping reunite families.

Although not immediately obvious with regard to agriculture, mobile phones are in fact making a huge difference in the lives of smallhold farmers. By serving as platforms for sharing weather information, as well as market prices, and micro-insurance schemes, mobile phones are allowing Africa's farmers to make better decisions, which then translate into higher-earning potentials.

Finally, let's look at health. Mobile phones are going to play an increasingly important role in improving the provision of healthcare to the citizens of African countries, not only helping individuals to locate health care providers more quickly, but making sure the drugs they use are genuine. The World Health Organisation estimates that nearly 30% of drugs supplied in developing countries are fake. A pioneering idea to put unique codes within scratch cards on medicine packaging means that buyers can now find out if the drug they are about to use is genuine or not. All they have to do is send the code via SMS to a designated number and find out. The system is now being used by several countries in Africa.

So, as we have seen, mobile phones have become not a luxury, but an affordable necessity which is undoubtedly improving the lives of individuals and changing the face of Africa.

Unit 8

For questions 1-14, choose the best answer a, b or c that answers each question appropriately.

1
Did you manage to put aside any money this month or have you spent it all?

2
Are you really going to apply for yet another credit card? Don't you think you've got enough already?

3

Joseph is having some cash flow problems. Can we lend him a hundred euros until he gets paid?

4

When do you think you'll get a pay rise?

5

Can you afford your loan repayments now that you've been made redundant?

6

How much profit have they made this month, do you know?

7

Do you mind if I give you the sales figures tomorrow?

8

Do you know when she's expecting to receive the end of year accounts?

9

Do you know if the sales figures are up this month?

10

How have your shares performed this year?

11

Which of these investments has provided the highest return?

12

Do you have to pay duty on gifts sent from abroad?

13

Do you realise how easy it would be to make a loss on this scheme?

14

I need some dollars for my trip to California. Do you know where I can get the best rate of exchange?

Unit 9

You will hear two people talking about the Damien Hirst exhibition at the Tate Modern in London. For questions 1-6, choose the best answer, a, b, c or d.

W   Have you been to the Damien Hirst exhibition at the Tate yet?

M   Yes, I went last week. I thought it was extraordinary.

W   Really? You did? Well, I'm not sure what to think. Actually, I'm not convinced the Tate should have put this exhibition on.

M   But surely he's one of the most influential and original artists alive today.

W   Mmm, maybe …

M   His work is so courageous and he really makes you think in a way that few other artists do.

W   Well, I agree that as a conceptual artist, he does have something to say, but I can't say I actually like his pieces. Where is the beauty?

M   Oh, I think there is plenty of beauty. His butterfly room is stunning, you know and calling it *In and Out of Love* is so clever, too. It's such a brilliant way of describing the fleeting nature of love. I think it's sheer genius.

W   And in the meantime thousands of butterflies have died on the floor of the Tate Museum. It's very cruel, I think, to keep butterflies in a white room without windows.

M   No, no! That's not the point at all.

W   Well, what is the point?

M   It's about love - the beauty of love and its fragility. I know there's been a lot of controversy about Hirst's butterflies. But in fact, he had an expert working for him who made sure they had the right living conditions and food and everything … They didn't suffer at all, you know.

W   That might well be the case, but these poor creatures never got to see a garden or a flower or feel fresh air. It's horrible, really.

M   I don't think you can really say that. They were warm and safe and had plenty of food.

W   If you say so, but that business of getting an expert in is typical, too. You do realise, don't you, that Damien Hirst doesn't actually make any of his own works? He just has the idea and then someone else does all the hard work. And then people pay him tons of money for them. It's ridiculous.

M   I don't think so at all. There has always been a tradition of great artists having assistants, from Leonardo da Vinci to Andy Warhol with his factory.

W   I'm sorry, but that's absurd. How can you compare them? Well, maybe you can compare him to Andy Warhol, but Leonardo?

M   Well, OK, maybe not Leonardo, but still you've got to admit, there is something brilliant about Hirst. His ideas might be simple, but nobody else has had them in quite the same way.

W   Well, he's certainly made a fortune out of them. He is Britain's richest artist after all …

M   Good for him! But you have to admit there is no one like him. He is unique.

W   Mmmm

M   Well, what about his diamond skull then? Not only is it stunningly beautiful, but it has so much to say about our world.

W   Why? Surely it's just a skull covered in priceless diamonds. Where's the skill in that?

M   Come on, you know there's much more going on than that! You've got to put it in a historical context, too. It's *Memento mori* art, an object that is supposed to remind you of your own mortality. It's something artists have been doing for centuries, and Hirst is doing just that, but by adding millions of pounds worth of diamonds, he's saying much more than you initially might think. In fact, you could say it embodies the spirit of our age.

W   Well, if you say so. I still thought the exhibition was quite unappealing, really … And don't get me started on his sharks in formaldehyde or his spot paintings, none of which he actually painted …

M   OK, OK, I can see I'm not going to change your mind …

Unit 10

You will hear five people talking about their lifestyles. Complete both tasks as you listen.

Task 1   For questions 1-5, choose from the list A-H the reason which best reflects why each person chose his or her current lifestyle.

Task 2   For questions 6-10, choose from the list A-H the main advantages of the lifestyles mentioned by each speaker.

Speaker 1
My greatest ambition in life had always been to become a journalist. I studied English language and literature at

university and edited the university student magazine. When I graduated, it took me a long time to get a job. I was relieved when I finally got one in a provincial newspaper and threw myself into the job, working very longs hours, six or even seven days a week. Little by little, though, I began to have doubts about my chosen profession. I just wasn't enjoying it as much as I'd hoped. A lot of the interviews I was doing seemed at best banal and at worst terribly intrusive. Finally, after a year, I handed in my notice. It was a big step, but I don't regret it for a minute. I decided to go back to college to train as a teacher. Now I work in a fantastic secondary school teaching English and this year, four of my students are following in my footsteps, going to my old college to study English language and literature. I'm so proud!

Speaker 2
On my fortieth birthday my life changed forever. I had been working in a bank, earning a good salary, for almost twenty years. I had everything you could ask for: a kind and devoted husband, three lovely children, a beautiful house in town, a cottage in the country, two dogs, two cars and a nanny. But everything I worked so hard for was being enjoyed by everyone else, except me. So, when I woke up on my fortieth birthday, I felt miserable. My husband and I talked about it for a long time and we decided that I would give up my job, we'd sell the house in town and one of the cars, give the nanny her notice, pack up the children and go and live in our cottage in the country. We've now been living here for three years and we all love it. We grow our own vegetables and are almost self-sufficient. The kids are much happier and so are my husband and I. We may have fewer things, but we have more time.

Speaker 3
I'd been made redundant and had been looking for a job for over a year. I was beginning to wonder if I'd ever work again when my sister Judy suggested we go into business together and open a café. I was very reluctant as I knew nothing about catering, but she persuaded me to take a risk. She'd been working in a restaurant for over a decade, but she needed someone to make sure the financial side worked and that's where I come in. It's been incredibly hard work, twelve to sixteen hours a day seven days a week. I feel we almost live there, but it's been worth it. We're making a small, but decent, profit and the future looks good again.

Speaker 4
Things hadn't gone quite as I'd anticipated. I always thought I'd get a well-paid job, buy a big house, send my kids to private schools. But my husband left me and there I was, a single mother of two, living in a small flat, struggling to make ends meet. I needed a way to make a living that would fit in with the kids and that's when I decided to take a risk and get a loan to buy a bigger house and take in lodgers. I was lucky my dad helped me with the loan, but he's really happy because it's paid off. I have three lodgers at a time. We all have our meals together and so far, I've been really lucky and we've all become friends. It's a brilliant way of making living – it's fun for the kids too – and at least one of my dreams has come true: I live in a big house!

Speaker 5
I wasn't very academic and didn't do that well in my exams, so my parents were quite worried when I left school at 16. I wasn't in the least bit worried, though, because I knew exactly what I wanted to do. I wanted to build houses and I was more than happy to start at the bottom and learn my trade. I was lucky enough to get an apprenticeship with a brilliant building company and they taught me every aspect of building a house. Now, twenty years later, I've got my own company. It's a great life. I'm my own boss, I have apprentices of my own, including my two sons, and I make a decent living.

Unit 11

You will hear three different extracts. For questions 1-6, choose the best answer, a, b or c. There are two questions for each extract.

Extract One
You hear two people talking about underwater hockey.

M So, Hannah, you've taken up underwater hockey. What's it like and are you enjoying it?

H Actually, Pete, I'm loving it. I had no idea there was such a thing as underwater hockey until I moved to New Zealand and they had competitions at my local pool.

M So you were a keen swimmer …

H That's right. I've always really enjoyed swimming and I used to be a member of a swimming club at school and at university. I did laps every morning before breakfast. And don't forget I was captain of the hockey team when I was in senior school.

M Yeah, I remember. You were really good. Your team were pretty unbeatable. But underwater hockey is a whole different ball game …

H You can say that again! The thing is, it's like hockey in that you've got a puck and the point of the game is to score goals. But you've got to do it underwater, at the bottom of a pool, wearing fins, a diving mask and snorkel, as well as a thick glove to protect your hand!

M That's crazy! But you must have to be very fit.

H Yes, and you have to be able to hold your breath for a long time. In fact, I practise holding my breath every day.

M Do you?

H Yeah, when I'm driving, I always do it then. When I get to a red light, I hold my breath until it turns green. It's great practice!

Extract Two
You hear part of an interview with a young tennis player.

W Steve, you're seventeen now and you've been playing tennis since you were three. Is that right?

M Yes, that's right. I don't know if it's a real memory, but they say I was obsessed from the moment my dad got me my first racket – that's what my parents say, anyway.

W So your dad's a tennis player too?

M Yes, but he was never professional. He didn't have the opportunities I've had. He started much later and although he was really, really good, he could never make it his whole life – he needed to go to work to earn money.

W But he's your coach, isn't he?

M Yes, he is. He's always been my coach, well except for a few months. But now he's given up his job and he's my coach full time.

W And isn't that quite difficult?

M Well, we thought it might be a problem. My mother was a bit worried. She thought we'd be on top of each other all the time and it would be too much. But actually, that hasn't been a problem. The thing is, at the end of the day, I know Dad will always have my best interests at heart and he knows how far he can push me and when I really need to have a break.

W	And I hear you've now got a fitness trainer as well.
M	Yes, that's Andy. He's been absolutely brilliant. I'm much stronger after just three months of weight training and my serve and my backhand have improved enormously.
W	Well, Steve, good luck! I hope we'll see you at Wimbledon next year.
M	Thanks. It's what I'm working for.

Extract Three
You hear part of an interview with a former Olympic rower.

W	So, Robin, how do you feel now that you've retired from rowing?
M	Well, I can't say I don't miss it, because obviously it was such a huge part of my life for so long, well over thirty years …
W	Yes, you started rowing at school, then university and then three Olympic Games.
M	Yes, a long time! In fact, I can hardly remember not having to get up at the crack of dawn and start the day with fitness training, or straight on to the river as the sun is rising.
W	So, how many hours a day were you training?
M	Well, it depended, of course. Before an important race, it would be eight hours a day, six days a week. But there were times when it would ease off and we'd train for four hours. Sometimes just in the gym, you know.
W	But it's the river you love, isn't it? You're famous for saying the River Thames was the love of your life!
M	Don't remind me! What a silly thing to say the week before your wedding. My wife has never let me forget it.
W	But on a more serious note, you've campaigned tirelessly to clean up our waterways and protect wildlife along our rivers.
M	Well, I'm very proud of my Clean River Campaign, I have to admit.
W	What about your gold medals? Surely they are your greatest achievements?
M	Well, I'm glad to have them. It was a great journey, but I would like to be remembered for my campaign, really.

Unit 12

You will hear someone talking about geothermal energy. For questions 1-8, complete the sentences.

The word geothermal comes from the Greek word 'geo', meaning earth, and 'thermos,' which means heat.

Geothermal energy (or 'earth heat' energy) is power from inside the Earth. It is thermal energy contained in the rock and fluids beneath the Earth's crust. It can be found from within shallow ground to several kilometres below the surface, as far down as the extremely hot molten rock called magma.

People have enjoyed geothermal energy for thousands of years by bathing in hot springs. Today these underground reservoirs of steam and hot water can be tapped to generate electricity or to heat and cool buildings directly.

Geothermal heat pumps can take advantage of the constant temperature of the upper three metres of the Earth's surface to heat a home in the winter, while they extract heat from the building and transfer it back to the relatively cooler ground in the summer.

Geothermal water from deeper in the Earth can be used directly for heating homes and offices, or for growing plants in greenhouses. Some U.S. cities pipe geothermal hot water under roads and pavements to melt snow.

To produce geothermal-generated electricity, wells at a depth of one and a half kilometres or more, are drilled into underground reservoirs to tap steam and very hot water that drive turbines linked to electricity generators.

Geothermal energy is generated in over twenty countries. The United States is the world's largest producer, and the largest geothermal development in the world is The Geysers north of San Francisco in California. Other countries which exploit geothermal power include Indonesia, Mexico, Italy, Japan and New Zealand.

Iceland is another. It has a population of just over three hundred thousand and is aiming to become self sufficient in renewable energy. It has at least twenty-five active volcanoes and many hot springs and as a result, over fifty percent of its energy comes from renewable geothermal energy and more than ninety-five percent of homes and buildings are heated this way.

Iceland is now looking for ways to export its geothermal energy in order to aid its economic recovery since the collapse of its banking industry in 2008. The Submarine Cable Project is a plan to connect Iceland to Europe via an underground cable allowing Iceland's excess geothermal power to be sold in Europe, where demand and prices for electricity are high. There is still a long way to go but one day, we might be using Iceland's geothermal energy to heat our homes in the UK.

National Geographic Learning, a part of Cengage Learning, is a leading provider of materials for English language teaching and learning throughout the world.
Visit National Geographic Learning online at **ngl.cengage.com**

ISBN 978-1-4080-6192-3

9 781408 061923

Second Edition

Kid's Box 6
Language Portfolio

Name: _____

Age: _____

School: _____

English and me

Karen Elliott
with Caroline Nixon
and Michael Tomlinson

CAMBRIDGE
UNIVERSITY PRESS

University Printing House, Cambridge CB2 8BS, United Kingdom

One Liberty Plaza, 20th Floor, New York, NY 10006, USA

477 Williamstown Road, Port Melbourne, VIC 3207, Australia

314–321, 3rd Floor, Plot 3, Splendor Forum, Jasola District Centre, New Delhi – 110025, India

79 Anson Road, #06–04/06, Singapore 079906

Cambridge University Press is part of the University of Cambridge.

It furthers the University's mission by disseminating knowledge in the pursuit of education, learning and research at the highest international levels of excellence.

www.cambridge.org
Information on this title: www.cambridge.org/9781107632295

© Cambridge University Press 2009, 2015

First published 2009
Second edition 2015

20 19 18 17 16 15 14 13 12 11 10 9 8 7 6 5

Printed in Great Britain by CPI Group (UK) Ltd. Croydon CRO 4YY

A catalogue record for this publication is available from the British Library

ISBN 978-1-107-63229-5 Language Portfolio 6
ISBN 978-1-107-66983-3 Pupil's Book 6
ISBN 978-1-107-63615-6 Activity Book with Online Resources 6
ISBN 978-1-107-65463-1 Teacher's Book 6
ISBN 978-1-107-64502-8 Class Audio CDs 6 (4 CDs)
ISBN 978-1-107-66629-0 Teacher's Resource Book with Online Audio 6
ISBN 978-1-107-66995-6 Interactive DVD with Teacher's Booklet 6
ISBN 978-1-107-43252-9 Presentation Plus 6
ISBN 978-1-107-69368-5 Posters 6
ISBN 978-1-107-68132-3 Tests CD-ROM and Audio CD 5-6

Additional resources for this publication at www.cambridge.org/kidsbox

Cambridge University Press has no responsibility for the persistence or accuracy of URLs for external or third-party internet websites referred to in this publication, and does not guarantee that any content on such websites is, or will remain, accurate or appropriate.